# The QUANTOCKS

## A PAST WORTH PRESERVING

Mary Siraut
Robert Dunning
Ken Brown

SOMERSET
BOOKS

First Published in Great Britain in 1992
by Somerset Books.

*British Library Cataloguing in
Publication Data.
CIP Catalogue Record for this book is
available from the British Library.*

ISBN: 1 897689 00 4

Somerset Books
Chinon Court
Lower Moor Way
TIVERTON. EX16 6SS.
Tel: 0884 243242
Fax: 0884 243325

*Designed for Somerset Books by:
Topics Visual Information
397 Topsham Road, Exeter, EX2 6HD.
Tel: 0392 876800.*

*Typeset by Icon, Exeter.*

*Printed and bound in Great Britain by
Sprint Print, Exeter.*

# ACKNOWLEDGEMENTS

The publishers gratefully acknowledge financial assistance from Somerset County Council, Friends of Quantock and Somerset Archaeological and Natural History Society towards the publication of this book.

**Friends of Quantock** was founded in 1949 to protect threatened deciduous woodland and to oppose large-scale afforestation. Since then it has expanded its role and tries to provide a voice for everyone who wishes to protect these beautiful hills.

Friends of Quantock leads walks and provides speakers for meetings. It has commissioned surveys of bracken, woodland and streams to monitor conditions and has financially helped tree planting, grass seeding, nest box installing, a deer survey and has repaired the ancient wall at Cothelstone. It also monitors planning applications, unauthorised vehicles, excessive noise, dumping, poaching and anything detrimental to the peaceful, natural beauty of the Quantock Hills.

Friends of Quantock, c/o Somerset Trust for Nature Conservation, Fyne Court, Broomfield, Taunton.

**Somerset Archaeological and Natural History Society** was founded in 1849 and is one of the oldest of its type in the British Isles as well as being the oldest in Somerset.

In addition to archaeology and natural history, it is also the centre for the study of local history and of historic buildings in the County and has published more than 130 volumes of Proceedings to make its work in these fields accessible to the public. The Society arranges a comprehensive programme of lectures, excursions, excavations, field meetings and social gatherings.

In 1873 the Society purchased Taunton Castle to save the historic site for Somerset. Here, its headquarters and library are housed, as well as the Museum, incorporating the Society's exhibits, which is leased to the County Council and is open free of charge to members

*Note:* The text of this book was originally delivered in the form of contributions to a symposium organised by the Somerset Archaeological and Natural History Society in Taunton in March 1990. They have been slightly amended and revised for publication.

# Contents

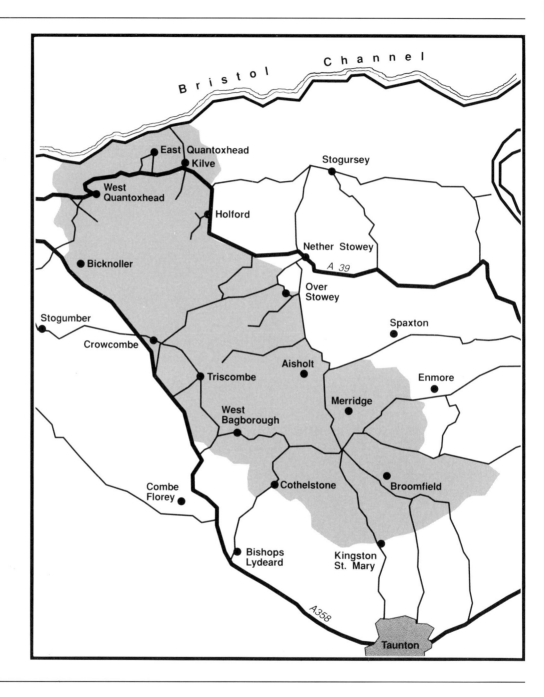

# Introduction

The history of the British landscape is the story of man's use and abuse, of natural resources sometimes over-exploited, of boundaries established and ignored, of customs broken; of livings scratched precariously, of profits made greedily over some six thousand years. Some places now remote bear witness to intense cultivation in the distant past; few places in our small island bear no trace of occupation at all.

In those same six thousand years the Quantocks have changed and changed again. A land searched by hunter-gatherers, settled by primitive farmers, hunted by Saxon warlords, carved up by conquerors. Its woods have been felled, coppiced, grubbed up; its open spaces ploughed; its streams harnessed, its tracks trodden or diverted; its lands emparked and enclosed, its people excluded. Its villages have been stable for at least two thousand years, but its hamlets and farmsteads have come and gone, often the results of migration or market forces.

So much has been lost – markets and fairs, broom squires, the Dodington Rit, the charcoal burner. Stag hunting is threatened, and so is the wild pony. In place of the grasping landlord, the thieving tenant and the perpetrators of various kinds of iniquity are the rhododendron, the poacher, the biker and the motor car. Change is inevitable, but destruction is surely not. This survey of the Quantocks, past and present, may serve to help in the appreciation of the past and the reasonable protection of the present.

*Wills Neck from the air. Some of the 'archaeology' is of the 20th century.*
S.C.C. ENVIRONMENT DEPT.

I

# In the Beginning

The Quantock Hills probably derive their name from the language of the Celts whose mark on our countryside is left in the names of most of our rivers and hills. The word 'cantuc' suggests the Welsh 'canto', meaning a circle or rim[1], a perfect description of the high ground stretching from the western end of the Somerset Levels to the Bristol Channel; a formidable barrier on the horizon of the advancing Saxons as they crossed the Parrett in the late seventh century. That barrier was soon reached and passed, but its value was recognised. Succeeding generations appreciated its natural riches, and the royal estate at Cannington, successor to an older political and perhaps religious focus, was known by its Saxon occupiers as 'Cantuctun'.

The hills form a ridge about 18 kilometres long and 5 kilometres wide. On the western side the scarp is often steep, but the slope is more gradual on the east. The highest point, called Wills Neck, is 384 metres above OD. At their northern end the hills are formed of Middle Devonian Hangman Grits. There are slates, sandstones, siltstones and some pockets of limestone in the central areas which geologists describe as Ilfracombe Beds. Nearer the Levels, in the southern area, the rock is called Morte Slate. Over these foundations the soils are a variety of red loam: acid and silty in the north, on the high, open moorland covered by heath and scrub oak; in the centre a mixture of open moorland, softwood plantations and enclosed hill pastures; in the south silty loams suitable for pasture.

This rich land has been long exploited. Mesolithic flints have been found among the scatters on the hills indicating the presence of hunters more than 6000 years ago. Leaf-shaped flint arrowheads, some perhaps fashioned on Cothelstone Hill and often found on the Quantocks, suggest that nomadic Neolithic man hunted in the area between *c.* 4000 BC and *c.* 2000 BC. The more sophisticated barbed-and-tanged arrowheads fitted to yew or hazel shafts and fired from yew bows were weapons of the Bronze Age, between *c.* 2000 BC and *c.* 700 BC, when men lived here a more settled life, probably choosing to site their rather ephemeral dwellings on the lower slopes near water, and burying their dead as guardians of their skyline.

These Bronze Age burial mounds, 'barrows' the Saxons called them, have thus long been a feature of the prehistory of the Quantocks. After a recent survey by Richard McDonnell[2], as many as 64 Bronze-Age round barrows and 46 flint sites have been recognised, suggesting a highly organised and long exploited landscape. Most of the barrows are stone cairns, the largest called Hurley Beacon, in part because of its later use as a beacon site. It is 25 metres in diameter and 2 metres high. A hollow in this and many other barrows indicates that it has been plundered. Among the barrows is one on Lydeard Hill used as a Saxon boundary marker called 'Rowbarrow', Thorncombe barrow above Bicknoller and others near Bicknoller Post and Wilmot's Pool. Two other barrows, one on Beacon Hill and one on Fire Beacon Hill, have had obvious later uses, and one on Cothelstone Hill was used as the site of a tower in the eighteenth century. These burials, it needs to be said, were not sited at random. Barrow cemeteries are often linear, presumably marking a boundary: in antiquity ancestors were guardians of family property.

The dwelling sites of the living are less easy to discover[3]. The hillforts and enclosures, usually thought to be of the Iron Age or later, were perhaps first established in the Bronze Age. Only further research and excavation can reveal the origin and development, for instance, of the newly-found settlement above Rams Combe, a complex of six circular platforms or depressions and enclosing defences. But hunt here Bronze Age man certainly did and (given the number of bronze artefacts found in the vicinity) perhaps he even extracted copper from the hills.

During the last thousand years BC the climate became cooler and wetter and, whether as a consequence or not, surviving monuments of the period change in character. By the millennium the people of the Quantocks came within the tribal area of the Dumnonii, less sophisticated than some of their neighbours for they bartered rather than using coin, but their hillforts and enclosures indicate a need for physical security.

Ramparts at strategically-placed sites leave clear traces, the best-known in the north called Dowsborough but earlier Dolesbery and Deuxbarrow, the last perhaps because someone recognised that there were two barrows within the later rampart. The later name Danesborough has confused many. Two other Quantock hillforts are at Plainsfield in Over Stowey and Ruborough in Broomfield, the latter named from the Saxon 'ruh burh', a fortress covered in natural vegetation. So had nature taken over when man abandoned.

Trendle Ring above Bicknoller and Higher Castles and Rooks Castle,

*Dowsborough hillfort, in Stringston ancient parish, looking north-west.*
S.C.C. ENVIRONMENT DEPT.

*Dead Woman's Ditch, Over Stowey, so named in 1782.*
S.C.C. ENVIRONMENT DEPT.

both in Broomfield, were enclosures more likely for stock than for military purposes despite the later names of the last two. They are the best known among nearly forty sites, some of which are further evidence that the Quantocks were exploited in the Iron Age. To them must be added the curious rampart known as Dead Woman's Ditch and other lesser linear earthworks on Higher Hare Knap and near Wills Neck. And, linking all, is the ridgeway, or rather two routes, joining together from the south and the east at Triscombe Stone, creating an almost indelible line across the hills, at once artery and boundary.

Roman interest in the Quantocks is difficult to demonstrate, but the hills were obviously within sight of the port at Combwich and the Romano-British landowner who in the third and fourth centuries occupied a six-roomed villa with mosaic floors, between the hills and the Parrett near the later settlement of Spaxton, probably grazed his stock on the hills. Other farmers fleeing from their homes around Ilchester in the later fourth century did not see the Quantocks as a place of safety for their wealth, but buried their hoards of coin further west. People with less to lose probably remained close to the land which had been home to their ancestors; waiting, if they only knew it, for the next wave of men to take over their land.

The Saxons, with their different customs, culture and language, abandoned the hillfort and the high enclosure for the village and the vale, leaving the open ground of the hills littered with traces of vanished cultures to be swallowed by nature and trodden underfoot. Cannington, once apparently tribal centre and perhaps early Christian shrine, became an estate of the West Saxon royal house, conveniently near an area so well suited to their favourite occupation of hunting.

*Triscombe Stone, the meeting place of tracks on the Quantock ridgeway.*
S.C.C. ENVIRONMENT DEPT.

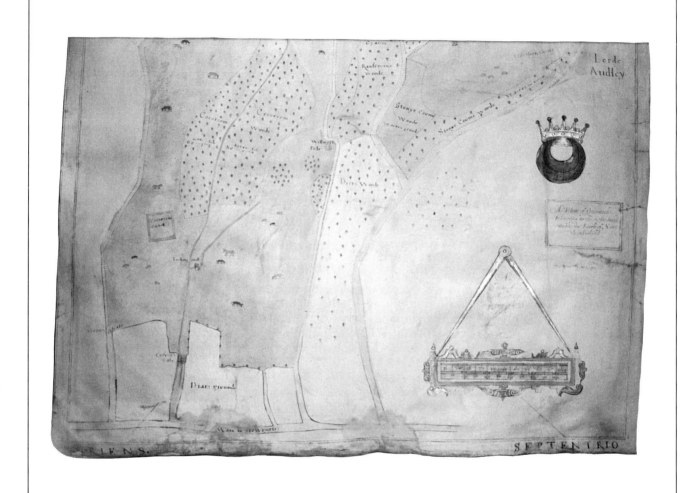

*'A plot of Quantock belonging to the right honourable the earle of Northumberland', 1609.*

# II

# Royal Forest to Private Domain

One of the oldest maps in the Somerset Record Office is one which actually belongs to the Archaeological Society.[4] It is entitled 'A plot of Quantock belonging to the right honourable the Earle of Northumberland'. To one side, highlighted in gold leaf, is an earl's coronet, above a black crescent, the badge of the Percy family. A fine scrolled cartouche surmounted by dividers in gold leaf includes the name of the London cartographer R. Treswell. The map is at first not too easy to place, but it portrays, with the help of a mass of rather stick-like horses and cattle in black or red, a large open grazing area with a pound, extensive tracts of woodland and a large square enclosure named 'Cocorcum Castle'. It shows, in fact, a large part of the parish of Over Stowey, some 1000 acres stretching south-east from West Hill above Rams Combe to Plainsfield and Aisholt hills.

Exactly how this map came into the Society's possession is not known, but for years it remained merely an interesting and valuable curiosity, a picture of a large tract of grazing land without the familiar furze or scrub and beech avenues which we now associate with that part of the countryside. What the Earl of Northumberland was doing so far from home was something of a puzzle which no doubt would one day become clear.

Some few years ago the Wiltshire Record Office acquired a volume then recently discovered in the attic of Maiden Bradley House, the home of the Duke of Somerset.[5] Illustrated with a number of detailed and fascinating maps, it is a survey of the estates of the Earl of Northumberland in Somerset, largely based around Stogursey. Among the maps is one of part of the Quantocks. Slightly smaller in scale than the first map, it has an elaborate border, compass rose and cartouche, without the name of the cartographer but bearing the characteristic style of the 'London' school to which Treswell belonged. The title of the map repeats in essence that of the first – 'The Platt of all Quantock in the County of Somersett being the inheritance of the right honorable the Earle of Northvmberland'. Overleaf there is a more significant addition – 'The Platt of Qvantock Parcell of the Manor of Weekfitzpaine'. The survey, according to its introduction, was made by Ralph Treswell in 1609, with additions to 1614. The maps are by Robert Norton.

How the volume came to be in the Duke of Somerset's attic is a consequence of the complications of the Percy family. In the later seventeenth century the family actually died out, for Joceline, the last earl, had but one surviving child, a daughter. Elizabeth Percy, a baroness in her own right, had three husbands. Her first, a Cavendish, she persuaded to change his name to Percy. Her second, a Thynne of Longleat and a friend of the Duke of Monmouth, was assassinated. Her third was Charles, the 'Proud' Duke of Somerset. The marriage caused a good deal of property, and the records to support their title, to change hands. Algernon, son and heir of Elizabeth and Charles, was seventh Duke of Somerset and first Earl of Northumberland of the second creation. He, too, had an only daughter, another Elizabeth, also Baroness Percy. Her husband, Sir Hugh Smithson, took little persuading to change his name to Percy on the promise of his wife's family earldom and estates. Yet somehow the Seymours retained many of the records. Some of them remained in Petworth House until very recently; the survey book eventually moved with the dukes of Somerset to Maiden Bradley.

All this may seem a long way from the Quantocks, but it actually explains why the full story of the Quantock Forest has not been told before. The medieval (and of course later) records of the manors of Stogursey, Wick FitzPayn and Wyndeats are to be found at Alnwick Castle, the West Sussex Record Office (the Petworth House material), the West Suffolk Record Office (MSS formerly at Hengrave Hill from another branch of the Percys) as well as in the Somerset Record Office and the Public Record Office in London.

And that full story is the clear identification of a Saxon royal forest. It is not a new idea; the Revd William Greswell, rector of Dodington and authority on Somerset forests at the turn of the century[6], put forward the claim, pointing to a curious phrase about a piece of land called Castle in Broomfield which seemed at the end of the thirteenth century to have been an offshoot of the royal manor of Somerton. The land in question was called *porcheria*, meaning a place where pigs were collected. He supported his assertion with some wild statements about moorland at Athelney and Durleigh which the Domesday commissioners had omitted, and some waste in Cannington hundred which seems to have been forgotten at the same time. After all this negative argument he also identified Newhall and Currill in Holford as tenements held until the eighteenth century in return for a rent representing payment in lieu of service at fawning time in Petherton Park. And, what was more, his own parish of Dodington was surely name after Dodo, the Domesday forester of Petherton?

Now those arguments by themselves did not prove all that convincing; but there was more land in Broomfield with interesting connections. Not far from that piggery at Castle, now known as Rooks Castle and still in the sixteenth century the common pound for the county, there was an estate called Kingshill, which paid rent to Somerton in 1204;[7] there was Kingslands, which belonged to the Crown before the Montacutes acquired it; Denesmodeswell (later Deadmanswell) and Oggshole, also anciently part of Somerton; and Melcombe, part of Creech manor and itself royal demesne in 1086 and until given away in Henry II's time. So that part of the Quantocks nearest the royal park of Petherton was clearly enough at some stage also royal.

Now let us move further along the ridge towards Dodington. It is just here that the Northumberland survey book reveals its value. According to the survey, there was attached to the manor of Wick FitzPayn in Stogursey a tract of land, then some 880 acres and called Quantock Common. It was described as 'wood and plain barren ground . . . . reputedly a quarter of Quantock Forest . . . . . by tradition [descending] from their ancestors'. Could that tradition, by then over 500 years old, have been wrong, or can the ownership be taken back from the real Percys of the early seventeenth century to Domesday? The answer is that the Percys inherited from the Poyningses, the Poyningses from the FitzPayns; the FitzPayns bought from the Crown, which held it for the mad Waleraunds, who inherited from the Nevilles of Essex, who could trace their line back to William de Curci (I) who married Emma, daughter and sole heir of William de Falaise, heir and probably son of that William de Falaise who held the great manor of Stoke in 1086.[8]

And it was this younger William de Falaise who between 1100 and 1107 granted to the monks of the Norman abbey of Lonlay 'pasture for their cattle in all places where he himself had pasture, and firewood as needed in his wood called Canthoc'.[9] That is a rather imprecise phrase, and considering Domesday Book makes no mention of a Falaise estate on the Quantocks, that reference might by itself prove doubtful. But John de Neville of Essex, lord of Stogursey, in the 1230s or 1240s gave to the nuns of Cannington 'sufficient wood for their hearth in my forest of Cantoke';[10] and in 1301, when the lunatic Robert Waleraund died, a survey of his estate mentioned 'wood on Quantock in which the prior of Stogursey, the prioress of Cannington, William of Gryndham, John de

Columbers and Margaret of Fairfield had grazing rights'.[11] So, surely, from Rook's Castle and the other Somerton connections in Broomfield through Over Stowey to Newhall and Currill, including, of course, Somerton wood in Kilve, there is evidence enough to claim the existence of a royal forest on Quantock.

How the lords of Stogursey managed their quarter share can be illustrated from the records not only at Alnwick and Petworth but others at Eton College and the Public Record Office. Some small pieces of land up there were cultivated by tenants who paid rent not in cash but in slabs of iron – nine sold for 18d in 1276-7[12] and 12 (amounting to 84lb in weight) for 4 shillings in the fifteenth century.[13] Heather was evidently cut and sold in the 1290s[14] when the manor of Wick employed a full-time reaper. Grass was cut for hay there in the 1480s which was carried home for storage in Stogursey castle and timber was felled in 1500-01 for house repairs and for two bressumers (beams) at the castle.[15]

The description of the wood where John de Columbers and Margaret of Fairfield had grazing rights in 1301 is a clue to another part of the Quantock story which still has consequences today. According to Domesday Book, ownership of the Quantocks was already a patchwork of lordships. Over Stowey, for instance, was divided between the foreign triumvirate of Alfred d'Epaignes, William de Falaise, and William de Mohun. So if Falaise had one quarter of the old forest, did not Alfred of Spain have a share too? Certainly the lordship which he held in Over Stowey descended to John de Columbers in the thirteenth century, to his successors, lords of Nether Stowey honor, until the seventeenth; and then to successive lords of Nether Stowey manor.

The land in question is the Stowey Customs – Robin Upright's Hill and Great Bear – where now the parish council of Over and Nether Stowey has registered common rights on behalf of all the householders, a claim based more on practice over many generations than on strict adherence to the law of lordship.

Alfred d'Epaignes was successor by 1086 to one particular estate called, like several others, simply Stowey, which in 1066 had a distinguished owner in the late Earl Harold of Wessex. Could this be anything to do with the royal forest and if so can the land be identified? In a charter by which Hugh de Bonville, one of the tenants of the Columbers estate in the mid twelfth century, gave land 'for the good of his soul' to God and the Apostle Peter and the church of Over Stowey, he described its bounds as best he might, beginning at a point which everyone would recognise, namely 'at Stawey harpet next to the old castle precinct'. Hugh's charter, copied into the cartulary of St Mark's Hospital, Bristol, is known,[16] but its significance has hardly been realised. Here in the mid twelfth century was an abandoned castle site. Now the

course of the roadway called 'Stawey harpet' is known: it runs at this point north of Over Stowey village, and a visit there will reveal the site, still a large, flat mound, an admirable spot for the dwelling of a lord. The Columbers family, feudal lords of Bonville's Over Stowey estate, had also become lords of Nether Stowey and had preferred to build on a new and strategically more sensible site further north-east, but the older site had been good enough for someone at an earlier date. Could it have been the castle of Earl Harold himself, and could it thus have been another relic of the royal forest of the Kings of Wessex?

Mention of the Stawey harpet is a reminder that the Quantocks have never been a significant barrier. The ridgeway which in prehistoric times delimited estates and was thus followed by medieval parish boundaries, was but one route of significance. The fact that it was in the seventeenth century the road to Taunton from East Quantoxhead, as shown on a map now at Court House, East Quantoxhead, is today the bane of the Quantock wardens, for motor cylists have as much right to use it still as any other. But might there be some further significance in the route adduced from the name by which part of it between West Bagborough and Over Stowey was known in the early fourteenth century – the Alferode.[17] The Revd Mr Greswell wanted to believe he heard echoes of the name Alfred there, but which Alfred, King or d'Epaignes?

*Robin Upright's Hill from the air, looking towards the sea.*
S.C.C. ENVIRONMENT DEPT.

15

*In Bicknoller village.*
ROBERT DUNNING.

The present valley road between Taunton and Williton below the Quantock scarp passed in its time for a road improvement, now following a lane, now cutting across ancient arable or pasture. The earlier route was on higher ground, running along the contour shared by Cothelstone, Bagborough and Crowcombe and ancient settlements between, like Triscombe and Halsway. Only Bicknoller is different and Bicknoller is a planned village, spread across a regular grid and mentioned in Domesday Book as Newton, new town. But Trendle Ring is also on that common contour. On the other side of the ridgeway many of the clues to the early road pattern were swept away in the nineteenth century when Henry Labouchere, later Lord Taunton, creating his magnificent Quantock Estate, obliterated Aley Green. But on this side the ancient settlements – Adscombe, Aley and Plainsfield – lie just where the ancient cross-ridge routes begin to run up their respective valleys: that up Adscombe to Seven Wells probably called 'the Great Way of Solmere' in the twelfth century,[18] and another from Aley to Triscombe.

The 'Stawey harpet' is of all these the most elusive but the most significant. Traced years ago, perhaps a little generously, by Mr Greswell as the route linking Bristol with North Devon, there is plenty of evidence for its course from the hillfort at Cannington to Swang and then south of Nether Stowey to the old castle precinct at Over Stowey – the name Stowey itself derived from the same 'stone way' and 'harpet' from the Saxon 'herpath' meaning military road. From the castle site it ran up

*Over Stowey castle, perhaps a stronghold of Earl Harold of Wessex.*
ROBERT DUNNING.

*Nether Stowey castle, stronghold of the Columbers family.*
S.C.C. ENVIRONMENT DEPT.

*Stogursey market place and priory church.*
S.C.C. ENVIRONMENT DEPT.

Great Bear to Crowcombe Park Gate, south along the ridgeway to Triscombe, and then down into the valley beyond. Its route before Cannington Hill is a little conjectural but the Parrett crossing at Combwich was important enough for much longer than this ancient route. For generations after putative soldiers tramped on its stones, the Parrett ferry was of significance, the life blood of places like Stogursey, whose success as a new town in the twelfth century depended on good communications. How good they proved to be is questionable – Stogursey never became the thriving metropolis which its founders doubtless hoped – but a road running westwards from there still bears the name Portway Lane as it winds its way between Fairfield and Holford, there to pick up that other cross-Quantock route, the Great Road or Hunting Path, for Watchet and Minehead and the sea routes beyond them; the same route which gave not only Stogursey people access to their share of the forest, but the tenants of Margaret of Fairfield in Stringston a path to their commons somewhere on the hill.

Mention of the market at Stogursey is a reminder that movement of people, goods and stock even over difficult terrain was constant. By 1301

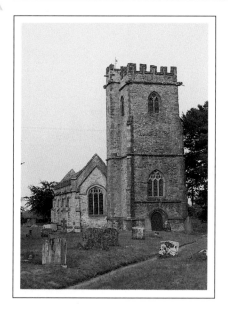

*Broomfield church from the west, showing the north aisle built in 1535.*
ROBERT DUNNING.

*Broomfield church: medieval glass fragments including the name of Alice Reskymmer, prioress of Buckland in the mid 15th century.*
ROBERT DUNNING.

*Crowcombe church from the south.*
S.C.C. ENVIRONMENT DEPT.

*Kingston St. Mary church, bench end featuring a pair of shears; early 16th century.*
ROBERT DUNNING.

*Spaxton church, bench end featuring a cloth worker; early 16th century.*
S.C.C. ENVIRONMENT DEPT.

there was a market at Stogursey every Saturday and a fair on St Andrew's Day each year. At the other end of the Quantocks there was a Monday market at Enmore after 1401 and a two-day fair around midsummer. In between, Broomfield had a three-day fair early in November from 1259, Crowcombe a Monday market from 1230 and a rival fair around All Saints Day from 1227; Nether Stowey a Tuesday market and a two-day fair early in September from 1304. No record of business at these gatherings survives, but the fact that they all outlasted the Middle Ages is of importance. So, too, is the possible claim to the oldest inn in Somerset, the tavern at Aley, perhaps the precursor of Parson Holland's drinking hovel on Aley Green, on the road between Taunton and Nether Stowey. It was there in 1201 and mentioned because Geoffrey de Malecombe was returning from it when he was murdered.[19] There was another, perhaps more respectable, hostelry at Broomfield by 1407, for Thomas Woth, its owner, left to Richard Bycombe all the 'necessary utensils' belonging to it, namely a basin, 6 pewter vessels, 6 pans, 2 crocks and brewing equipment.[20]

Another measure of Quantock prosperity is the interest of ecclesiastical land owners in its soil, for the Church would not be found investing in unprofitable land, and what secular donor would seek to save his soul with an unworthy gift? Between about 1155 and 1181 Hugh de Bonville endowed Over Stowey church and then gave it to Stogursey Priory. The priory exchanged it with Bishop Jocelin in 1239 for a more certain annuity and in 1326 Bishop Droxford gave its land but not the advowson to St Mark's Hospital, Bristol. St John's Hospital, Bridgwater, had land at Adscombe by 1220 and later built a chapel there; and Athelney Abbey enjoyed an income from Adscombe, too, which went to support the convent kitchen. Athelney also had land at Broomfield, and so did Buckland Priory, the latter owning the church by 1314 after an earlier attempt to make it a prebend of Wells Cathedral had failed. If all that sounds remote, yet until the nineteenth century the parish was still considered a Peculiar of the Dean of Wells, and there is still some glass in the church recalling Alice Reskymmer, prioress of Buckland in the mid fifteenth century. Taunton Priory owned Kingshill in Broomfield, some land at Stringston and the manor of Thurloxton, given first by 1258 for the support of the convent pittancer but later shared between five of the priory's officials. The Dean and Chapter of Wells acquired Bicknoller in the 1330s.

From church estates to churches is but a short distance. It will not be profitable to suggest which might be the oldest church on the Quantocks, for arguments will rest on the survival of identifiable fabrics or documents and not on foundations. Parish boundaries and other evidence, however, suggest that the area formed parts of at least four

*Photograph of Aisholt church about 1860 by Robert Gillo of Bridgwater.*

pre-Conquest minster parishes based at North Petherton, Stogumber, Nether Stowey and Spaxton. Surviving fabrics vary widely in date during the Middle Ages. There is a late Norman south doorway at Enmore and essentially twelfth century fabrics at Thurloxton, Over Stowey, Cothelstone, Bicknoller and Broomfield. Each was later to be transformed when piety and prosperity could be induced to come together, Broomfield's north aisle actually built in 1535.[21] Prosperity if not piety is certainly apparent in the fourteenth century at Crowcombe, Enmore, Thurloxton and Over Stowey, in the fifteenth at Aisholt, and in the later fifteenth or the sixteenth century at Bicknoller, West Bagborough, Kingston St Mary and Crowcombe.

It was a prosperity based not just on exploiting the soil in various ways. The Quantocks have a long and distinguished industrial history, in medieval times dating back to the slabs of iron paid by tenants at Lexworthy in Enmore in 1086 and the iron rents from Over Stowey in the late thirteenth century. Cloth production, so clearly portrayed in the bench ends at Kingston St Mary and Spaxton, was widespread, with fulling mills at Nailscombe in Broomfield, Thurloxton, Adscombe, Plainsfield, Crowcombe and elsewhere. One other industrial enterprise, taking advantage of natural resources, was pottery manufacture. The potters who paid 20 shillings in 1275 for the right to work in Nether Stowey have long been known, and in 1969 a kiln and thirteenth century potsherds were found in Portery Field south of Nether Stowey Castle. But the business, like the available raw material, was more widespread. Take, for example, Robert Wilcocks of Stogursey, 'called le Potter', who in the 1370s held a burgage and half an acre in Stogursey borough and who found himself arraigned as a pledge in Fairfield manor court in 1386.[22] The clay deposit he found so essential was still being used, or rather misused, by four miscreants reported at the manor court of Durborough in 1446[23] for leaving open claypits after their diggings in contravention of agreements; while a fellow, John Webber (how misleading a surname can be), was ordered to be arrested for selling pots 'against the custom of the manor'. All five men were still ignoring the court two years later, Webber still accused of selling pots and other earthenware vessels in the countryside, while another offender, his own son John, had been employing men for six years 'by day and by week' and John Hale had employed his own son, then aged 15, for at least three years in the business.

Although agriculture was the essential support of everyday life in the Quantocks as elsewhere in the Middle Ages, the records of the exploitation of land by traditional cultivation have left relatively few traces. The apparently precise statistics of Domesday book are dangerous; was there only one pig at Thurloxton in 1086, or only one pig on the lord's farm?

*Traces of the past near Tetton.*
S.C.C. ENVIRONMENT DEPT.

The traditional large open arable fields were inappropriate on the steep land of the Quantocks, but two farms in Broomfield, Duckspool and Binfords, seem to have had 'in' fields, and therefore presumably 'out' fields, and there was evidently common arable on the lower and more level ground, notably at Crowcombe, and meadow and pasture were grazed on community lines. Thus in Spaxton there was a custom about securing haycocks after gleaning in the fifteenth century; woodland grazing for pigs was practised in Enmore in the thirteenth century, and the grazing of common pasture there in 1261 caused disputes. By the end of the Middle Ages, in fact, most of the former common land had been divided into the small enclosures which are so familiar today, though some of the equally familiar open or wooded land, such as Buncombe Hill, was divided into small arable plots, while other areas were covered by furze and heath. In Spaxton in the thirteenth century and in Bicknoller in the 1330s water leats were constructed to take full advantage of an abundant rainfall.

By the end of the Middle Ages, too, many of the familiar farms had been created, often by free tenants who carved them out, like Roebuck, Cooksley and Water farms in Crowcombe, well away from the villages on the parish boundary. Those tenants, mostly nameless, were successors to others who, a century and more earlier, 'were dead of the plague', leaving the lord of Crowcombe Biccombe manor with a considerable drop in income. The lords of Quantock manors are at least known by name, and so are some of the late-medieval gentlemen who were the successors to the great lords of Domesday. What they have left behind include the parks at Aisholt and Aley, the latter broken into in 1327 by 36 people, who hunted deer there and killed a foal and some cattle.[24]

*Court Farm, Spaxton, probably the home of Robert Hill in the 15th century.*
ROBERT DUNNING.

More obvious traces of ownership are the houses in which they lived. There are still plenty of traces of medieval origins in many houses on the Quantocks, and documentary evidence for many others. There was, for instance, a substantial manorial complex at Plainsfield in the fifteenth century which included the house and farm buildings, a chapel, and a gatehouse.[25] The name Stonehall at Enmore, mentioned in 1455,[26] is surely in itself significant, and Tirelands and Barford in the same parish were standing at the same period, the former still revealing its essentially medieval character. Behind the church at Spaxton is another such house. Court Farm is an L-shaped building with late-medieval doorways and cross-passages in each wing and traces of other entrances as well. Inside all is gutted of anything significant – no hall, no parlour to be recognised. And yet it was in the early fifteenth century the home of Robert Hill, lord of Spaxton and Aley and Perry Fichet and Postridge and of much else besides; successor, in his more modest way, to Alfred d'Epaignes and William de Falaise. His house only makes sense if it is seen not simply as a home but as a staff headquarters, for an estate which spread over the Quantocks and stretched between Cornwall and Berkshire, needed, as his successor's records show, a significant staff.[27] Stewards, receivers, bailiffs, collectors and messengers, crossing and re-crossing the Quantock ridge on their lawful occasions, stand as an example of the care and concern for their country which Quantock people showed in the Middle Ages.

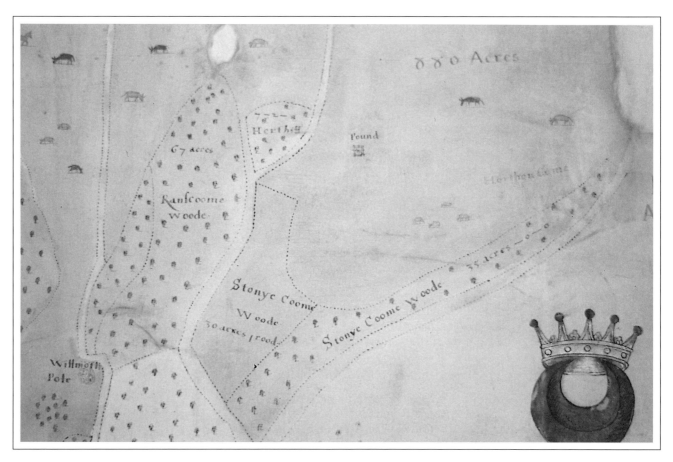

*The 'plot of Quantock', detail.*

# III

# The Land Exploited

By the end of the Middle Ages settlement around the Quantocks was well-established, even remote sites in the valleys and hollows in the hills being occupied until narrow tracks, steep hillsides and smallholdings became too much of a challenge to motor vehicles, tractors and the market economy.

Although arable land may have dictated the layout of settlement in the Saxon and Medieval periods no estate could thrive without a balance of arable, meadow and pasture land. The animals that drew the plough and the cart needed grass and hay and any restriction on meadow and pasture imposed severe limits on the amount of arable that could be cropped. At Broomfield an expansion in the arable may have been partly responsible for the improvement of the balls or large downs, often under furze and heath, which had been cleared by the end of the Middle Ages, like some of the woodland, for pasture. At Bicknoller disputes over the commons in the sixteenth century led to complaints of farmers forcibly rescuing impounded animals.[28] Parishes without adequate pasture remained impoverished and these effects could linger into modern times as at Over Stowey, the poorest parish in the area in the nineteenth century, possibly due in part to the inhabitants' historic lack of legal access to the hills. The high ground to the west and north-west of the parish was shared throughout the Middle Ages and later between the honors and lordships of Stogursey and Nether Stowey. The Stogursey share was partly wooded and partly open ground and was common to the tenants of Wick Fitzpayn manor. In the sixteenth century the manor derived a large part of its income from the exploitation of this land including payments for pasture, pannage of pigs in the woodland and the tillage of small areas to grow rye and oats, besides fines for strays and illegal pasturing and sales of wood. The bounds of the common were carefully laid out following roads, gates and hedges and perambulated from time to time, with the manor court keeping a careful record. Some of the points on the boundary can still be recognized today.

Use of the commons was regulated in the sixteenth and early seventeenth centuries by courts of survey which laid out the customs binding on the tenants. The Northumberland survey book[29] was compiled from such a court held in James I's reign but drawing on orders and customs laid down in earlier surveys. In 1564, for example, it was ordered that the Quantock commons be chased (i.e. the animals rounded up) twice a year and that all strays be impounded until valued. They were then to be taken to Wick Park in Stogursey for a year and a day, presumably to allow their owners to raise the fine for recovering them, and any remaining at the end of the period were to be sold to the profit of the manor. The manor courts appointed a hayward who was responsible for rounding up the strays and impounding them. The lord of the manor built and maintained a pound on the hills. There was some resentment among the tenants of Wick manor, who each had the right to put 30 sheep on the hills, against tenants of Crowcombe and Plainsfield manors who had been pasturing their animals on the commons for at least two centuries on payment to the lord of Wick manor who was clearly reluctant to forego the regular income this produced. In the early seventeenth century orders were made governing the grazing of woodland areas. Cattle were forbidden to feed in copses and were not allowed to graze in felled woodland for seven years after the trees were cut down, presumably to allow the wood to regenerate. Tenants taking leases of woodland were allowed to enclose them with ditches.

Each tenant of Wick manor was allowed to break the soil of the hill commons for crops under the supervision of the bailiff for a charge of 1 shilling an acre for rye and 6 pence an acre for oats. Temporary cultivation of rye plots on the hills was common in many parishes on both sides of the Quantocks. It was most frequently recorded in the sixteenth and seventeenth centuries when it was carefully regulated by the various manor courts which collected small payments for each plot. Plots were usually cultivated once every five or ten years. Small areas of common land on high ground, such as a plot of 14 acres on Buncombe Hill in 1515, were thus brought under temporary cultivation and in 1593 tenants of Broomfield manor had to hedge their hill plots within three weeks of sowing.[30] At Aisholt during the 1590s small areas on Aisholt and Hawkridge hills were broken for tillage on payment of only 1 penny an acre to the lord and in 1602 about 23 acres of common were under cultivation.[31] In 1603 hill land was let out for rye-growing at Merridge.[32] The enclosures and plough furrows can still be seen on aerial photographs of the open upland areas. Encroachments on the commons for tillage were sometimes followed by squatter settlement especially in the seventeenth century in the combes and along the roadsides on both sides of the Quantocks. Cottages were sometimes allowed by the manors and by Quarter Sessions in cases of hardship but illegal homes, little more than hovels, continued to encroach on to the hill areas until the nineteenth century.

By the seventeenth century the old manorial system was beginning to crumble and smaller landowners and the larger tenant farmers began to assert themselves against the declining power of the great and usually absent landlords. In the 1630s at least 180 acres, part of Plainsfield Hill, was divided and allotted to local landowners including the lord of Plainsfield manor in return for the surrender of their claims to common over the whole area.[33] By 1683, and probably by 1656, about half the remainder of the Stogursey land had been enclosed and let, and Quantock farm was created soon after 1686.[34] The owner, Robert Siderfin, probably built the wall which marks the western boundary of both the farm and the parish and which once bore his name.

*Quantock farm, Over Stowey.*
S.C.C. ENVIRONMENT DEPT.

The Nether Stowey share of the hills, known as the Stowey Customs and covering Robin Upright's Hill and Great Bear, remains largely unenclosed, although Warren House, recorded in 1672, had become the centre of a small farm by 1838. Attempts to enclose the area in the 1800s led to disputes between the lord of Nether Stowey and the vicar of Over Stowey, William Holland, the latter claiming the right to cut wood there. In 1803 the vicar was informed that Mr Symes, a lawyer, would be bringing an action against him for cutting wood in Custom Wood which was being enclosed for Mr Balch, lord of Nether Stowey. The vicar stated in his diary: 'I am well prepared for him having cut myself for above twenty years and I can prove the cutting out of the Custom Wood in lieu of Tithe for above a hundred years back.' The case dragged on and in 1807 the vicar declared: 'This is a dirty business of Richard Symes who puts money into his pocket and must take mine whether I gain the Cause or not. These Lawyers are bad animals in the community.' Holland won his case but the matter took a while to settle, leading to social diffculties: 'we were all to go and drink tea at Mr Symes's but I declined it. Mr Symes has brought an Action against me for cutting wood on Quantock which he has failed in and withdrawn yet no settlement has been made on the Occasion for which reason I cannot go to his House to drink tea. However he and his wife came over and begged and entreated me to come but I kept firm.' The vicar made use of his rights in subsequent years and in 1810 recorded that his servants cut half a hundred of the finest wood: 'It was a great load for one horse and they first had to carry it on their backs and afterwards the horse drew it as far as the road in two divisions and then it was put together and carried home, a great undertaking indeed for men and horse. By this means I get wood very cheap, not above 3 shillings per 100 and it is worth a guinea a hundred and moreover it exercises my right on Quantock.'[35]

The exploitation of the hill common land at Over Stowey is better documented than in other areas but similar practices occurred elsewhere. Tenants at Merridge had rights on Merridge Hill including pasturing cattle, cutting fuel and digging for stones, and these were confirmed in 1837 after a dispute with Edward Esdaile, lord of the manor of Merridge.[36]

Field and farm names throughout the area indicate the clearance of woodland. Much of the hill area, especially the eastern slopes, was well wooded and although landlords reserved large tracts of wood for their own use there were substantial areas of common woodland. Bark from woodland at Crowcombe was used by local tanners in the seventeenth century, one of them leasing 40 acres of wood for the purpose. In 1725 the bark was sold from 500 oaks felled to build Crowcombe Court.[37] Across the Quantocks at Kilton much of the woodland was treated as common.

*Left: Holford Beeches beside the Great Road.*
S.C.C. ENVIRONMENT DEPT.

*Crowcombe Court; wash drawing by J. Buckler, 1835.*
SOMERSET ARCHAEOLOGICAL SOCIETY.

Customary tenants had the right to cut spars, faggots, and underwood except oak, ash or crab apple but they might root up apples for transplanting into their own orchards and cut timber for essential repairs to their properties. As in many parishes tenants were allowed to cut and sell elm on their holdings. Elm was sometimes described as the 'weed of the district'; times have changed. At Broomfield in 1580 there were trees or underwood on Buncombe Hill, Broomfield Common and Lyeforde and 'great woods' called East and West Broomfield and West Churchmans woods.

Some clearances had taken place by 1653 and more in the east at Patcombe and Rooks Castle in the mid eighteenth century[38] but in the early nineteenth planting was carried out at Kingshill, Priors Down and

*Oak coppice, Great Bear.*

S.C.C. ENVIRONMENT DEPT.

elsewhere, giving a total of around 500 acres, mainly coppice wood, in Broomfield parish in 1838. By 1905 the area had increased to nearly 600 acres and although Priors Down and Kingshill had been cleared Buncombe Hill and Broomfield Common were well covered.

Illegal felling on the hills has been a constant problem down the ages and offenders were frequently prosecuted in the manor courts. Few, however, can have been quite as bold as William Mullins and his cronies who stole wood from the Earl of Northumberland's estates on the Quantocks in 1662 as revealed by the earl's local agent John Day of Knighton in Stogursey: 'William Mullins of Bagborough is building of a house in the highway and he hath stolen from my lord's wood three score and fourteen oaken rafters and lastes and three or four alders.' These were just the timbers Day had managed to seize; Mullins had been aided by another man and a boy.[39]

Woodland management can be traced from the later sixteenth century. Copyholders at Broomfield had the rights to shrouds of trees in certain areas, and in 1580 a proportion of the shrouds on Buncombe Hill and other places was let in return for manuring and tillage and later some small-scale felling. Broom was also sold. Coppicing was carried out near Binfords in the early eighteenth century, and felling at Buncombe c.1815 produced 516 oaks.[40] Timber from Broomfield was used to build two vessels at Bridgwater c. 1878 and continued to be exploited at the beginning of the twentieth century.[41] The woodland provided employment for a significant number of carpenters in the later nineteenth century. Over Stowey by contrast seems to have suffered from poor woodland management. In 1640 a tenant had cut down and sold 13 acres of wood without permission and was growing corn on the land. At this period wood sold for 5 marks (£3 6s. 8d.) an acre, a substantial sum and clearly a temptation. Woodland on the lower slopes belonging to the Over Stowey rectory estate had largely disappeared by 1655 and what remained was scrub rather than timber. In 1739 only half Parsonage Wood was actually timbered and the trees, six years old or less, were decayed. Friarn wood was said to cover 220 acres in the mid seventeenth century but by 1688, 46 acres had been 'lately grubbed up' and the remainder was coppice.[42] At about the same time half of the newly-created Quantock farm was woodland fit for sale, but by the late eighteenth century most of the wood there was fit only for coppicing. By the end of the nineteenth century firs had been planted widely on E.J. Stanley's Quantock Estate, a policy which was continued in the twentieth century by the Forestry Commission despite local protest. In 1905 there were 920 acres of woodland in Over Stowey parish. Clear felling took place during the First World War but replanting started in 1922. On the Duke of Buckingham's estates in Holford and Dodington 100 000 trees

*Binfords, Broomfield 1756.*
SOMERSET COUNTY LIBRARY.

were planted each year in the early nineteenth century and woodland was managed both for coppicing and for timber. Former commons were enclosed, common rights extinguished and the land planted with trees. Large areas of the Quantocks remain wooded in the late twentieth century and are now used as an amenity area for recreation as well as for commercial purposes.

Woodland did not only supply timber and fuel but also bark for tanning and small wood for charcoal making. As most of the woodland in Over Stowey parish was oak coppice by the eighteenth century it was used to provide bark, poles, faggots and charcoal. John Walford, the murderer whose gibbet became a local landmark, was, like his father before him, a charcoal burner in Over Stowey. It was a strange isolated life as Walford spent the winter in a hut on the hills, only coming down at weekends. The scrubby areas provided furze for kindling, materials for broom making, and of course, whortleberries. Collecting the latter formed an important source of income for the poor, especially landless labourers who relied on the income each autumn to pay their rent or buy clothes.

At East Quantoxhead unlicensed removal of furze, stones and turf from the commons was complained of. Heath burning and turf cutting were regulated by the manor courts. Tenants were given the right to a fixed number of turves per year or the amount a man could cut in two days. William Holland recounts how the poor women of his parish went out on the hills to cut heath. Although it was only April they were naked except for a flannel petticoat, probably because they could not afford to get their clothes torn. They covered themselves with bundles of heather when the vicar passed. He also had dealings with the broomers in the early nineteenth century. While riding on the hills in 1812 he saw a group of broomers making an enclosure beside the Crowcombe road to plant potatoes. 'Know you said I that I must have tithe. We intend it answered they. They told me the Palmers (a brooming family) were sent to jail for stealing wood.'

Riding out the next year Holland met Thomas Palmer, one of the broomers who had been unwilling to pay his tithes on the enclosure but had eventually paid up: 'I called to him – Now you begin to pay your tithe you'll have a good crop and prosper. He smiled and said he hoped he would. An elderly woman in the field said I do not grudge it at all for you be a Good kind of Gentleman.'

Holland also disapproved of the changes in farming in his admittedly backward parish and in particular of the reorganization of farms on Lord Egmont's estates and the eviction of small tenant farmers in 1809 by Mr Cruikshanks the steward: 'He will at this rate soon depopulate the parish for he turns out all the smaller tenants and the houses are going to decay and we shall soon have nothing but labourers and beggars in the Parish'.[43] In 1838 there were about 57 landless cottages in Over Stowey parish of which 37 were built on roadside waste,[44] some little more than huts on the roads to the hills which provided them with subsistence in the form of materials for brooming, berries and firewood.

In 1843 the Parliamentary Commissioners investigating the employment of women and children in agriculture reported on the labouring population that 'considering the scantiness of their diet and their insufficient clothing; their health and strength of body, their activity of mind and contented cheerfulness, are . . . surprising'.[45] In 1851 17 men, nearly all members of one family, were broomers living in areas with easy access to the Stowey Customs, the only part of the parish which remained common land. By this date almost half the acreage of Over Stowey parish was the personal property of Henry Labouchere, later Lord Taunton, and was reserved for his exclusive occupation.

Another group of Parliamentary Commissioners reporting in the late 1860s interviewed Lord Taunton's agent about the broomers. He described them as squatters owning their own cottages, with very large families living in one room. They took heather (he described it as stealing) from the moors and poles from the coverts and sold their brooms in Bridgwater, but the demand for them was declining. About a dozen cottages at Castle Hill were occupied by broom squire families. Most of the children attended school but the men did not adapt well to labouring. Labourers on the farms received between 9 shillings and 10 shillings with cider. New cottages were being built, but with only one room and a tiny back kitchen containing a copper. Stairs at the back of the room led to two or three very small bedrooms, little more than sleeping lofts, under a sloping roof. Each cottage had a pigsty and a privy at the bottom of the garden. The agent admitted the cottages were too small but few improvements in housing appeared until the twentieth century and poverty remained a problem. Many left the area in search of work in the later nineteenth century but the broom squires remained a feature of parish life.[46]

However, not all the inhabitants of the Quantock hills were poor. Many farmers did well and landowners had for centuries used every means to maximise their incomes from the land. In 1641 Richard Lawrence of Pepperhill in Over Stowey died a relatively wealthy man, certainly one of the most comfortably housed in the parish, with goods, crops, cattle and sheep valued at nearly £300. He had his own brewhouse and probably made his own cheese and candles. His house was well furnished by local standards and he owned a quantity of silverware.[47] Two hundred years later and scarcely half a mile away, Henry Labouchere, Lord Taunton, was living in considerable style in his new baronial mansion at Quantock

*Quantock Lodge, designed for Henry Labouchere, Lord Taunton, by Henry Clutton; begun 1857.*
SOMERSET COUNTY LIBRARY.

Lodge, and Pepperhill had become his home farm and dairy. More than 20 indoor servants were employed, excluding the family's personal attendants, and outdoor staff included a gamekeeper with 8 assistants.

The reduction of arable on the uplands and the development of pleasure grounds and plantations by the early nineteenth century probably helped to facilitate the re-introduction of the red deer from Exmoor in the mid nineteenth century by Edward J. Esdaile of Cothelstone. He released three hinds from Dulverton in Cockercombe in 1839, a practice which he and others continued for many years although not all the forced immigrants were willing to stay and some made their way back to Exmoor.[48] Eventually, however, a sufficient number had established themselves for hunting to be started in 1865, but regular hunting on the Quantocks did not begin until the Quantock Staghounds were established in 1901.

*Cothelstone House, from a drawing by J.P. Neale, c.1882.*
SOMERSET COUNTY LIBRARY.

Water was another exploited resource not only for domestic use and watering livestock but as a source of power for grain, fulling and blade mills, and as an indispensable part of the tanning and dyeing industries. There were at least four grain mills and one fulling mill in Broomfield; one of the mills, near the boundary with Kingston, was extended during the sixteenth century to form a complex of three mills. There was a mill at Merridge from the thirteenth to the eighteenth centuries and streams running down from the hills powered as many as 11 grist mills, 5 fulling mills and a blade factory in Spaxton parish alone. Mills at Cannington, Stogursey, North Petherton and many other parishes drew their power from water flowing off the Quantock Hills. At Over Stowey the many streams drove three grist mills, a blade mill and at least six fulling mills. Adscombe mill was said never to want water although it had no pond

*Combe House Hotel, Holford, formerly a tannery.*
S.C.C. ENVIRONMENT DEPT.

and the enterprising miller's assistant rode round the parish collecting small quantities of grain for milling in the later seventeenth century and was accused of unfair tactics by other millers whose customers he ruthlessly poached.[49] The most important site was at Marsh Mills which was a seventeenth century fulling mill occupied by a clothier who probably carried out dyeing and finishing of cloth on the premises. His successors took to tanning instead, but the mill was rebuilt between 1812 and 1816 as a silk mill, supplied with water by a new canal which can still be seen. The clerk of the mill came down from Cheshire, probably from the Macclesfield area, which was an important centre of silk weaving, and by 1817 a large number of women were employed at the mill. William Holland complained that they attended Methodist meetings where 'sad work there is, I am told, between the young men

*Crowcombe Court, built for Thomas Carew by Thomas Parker and Nathaniel Ireson, c.1725–39.*
S.C.C. ENVIRONMENT DEPT.

*Barford House, Enmore, built in the early 18th century.*
S.C.C. ENVIRONMENT DEPT.

and them.'[50] The silk mill ceased work during the late 1830s and was later converted to a grist mill. These streams, each one in the past with several mills along its length, now supply the reservoirs at Hawkridge, Ashford and Durleigh, the modern contribution to the exploitation of resources provided by the Quantock hills.

Clothmaking was a vital industry from the late Middle Ages until the end of the seventeenth century. The rural cloth industry was scattered throughout most of the parishes; there were few large-scale businesses, and most cloth was made part-time at home for clothiers who provided the raw materials and paid for the finished work. Fulling and dyeing required good sources of water and there was plenty of local wool. Most fulling mills were established by clothiers who had capital to build and equip them. Wool and yarn were put out to carders, spinners and weavers but some rural clothiers did their own dyeing and finishing. At Pepperhill there were racks for drying and stretching cloth and there was a dyehouse in a nearby combe in the sixteenth century. An Over Stowey clothier was accused of over stretching his cloth and using inferior materials in 1631.[51] Theft of materials is often recorded: one clothier was accused of stealing red or ginger coloured cloth from another clothier's rack in 1671.[52] Spaxton parish was a centre of clothworking at this period, notably by the Collard family who moved from Taunton and were prominent in Spaxton throughout the seventeenth century. As late as the end of the seventeenth century clothiers were at work in Holford. Lewis Pollard died in 1688 a wealthy man whose equipment and quantities of both raw and finished materials indicate organized production.[53] Flax was grown in some of the combes and linen was produced in the early eighteenth century at Holford and Kilve. Flax growing was revived locally during the Napoleonic Wars when local farmers were encouraged to supply flax for the Navy.

The availability of bark, water and hides led to a thriving tanning industry the most well-known being those at Holford and Nether Stowey. Smaller tanneries existed in Over Stowey during the eighteenth century. A tanyard at Bincombe in 1716 had a large and varied stock of leather including 111 calfskins, a large quantity of bark and several vats and troughs.[54] There was also a tanyard at Marsh Mills kept by the Poole family, relatives of Thomas Poole the famous Nether Stowey tanner and patron of literary men. Tanning was unpopular and the Nether Stowey tannery was unusual in being sited in the heart of the village. The smells and the pollution of the streams used by many to draw their drinking water and wash their linen was a constant source of complaint. Thomas Poole's tannery included a barkhouse which survives, now converted into a private house, and was in existence for over a century supplying the needs of many local glovers, saddlers and shoemakers. A tanyard

*Thomas Poole (1765-1837), businessman and patron of literature.*

south of Four Forks, Spaxton, was in business during the nineteenth century and in 1832 produced 30 hides a week. The largest tannery, however, was that at Holford Combe. By the mid nineteenth century the complex included a bark mill, tan pits, glue house, carpenter's shop and counting house. The business continued into the early twentieth century and the great iron wheel which provided power still survives, although the tannery has been converted into a hotel.[56]

The geological structure of the Quantocks including marls, sandstones, slates, grits and limestones has provided a further source of income down the ages. Quarries for limestone and tilestones operated at Rooks Castle in the fourteenth century and at Nailscombe in the sixteenth. On the western side of the Quantocks tile stones were quarried at Crowcombe in the sixteenth and seventeenth centuries and limestone dug for stone and lime to build Crowcombe Court in 1725. The bricks for the Court and the Rectory were also made locally.[57] In the seventeenth century there was some illegal quarrying at Broomfield and lime was being sold without leave of the manor court. There were limekilns in the parish throughout the eighteenth and early nineteenth centuries, especially at Holwell where a unique cavern contains anthodites, clusters of aragonite formed at the meeting point of slate and limestone. Stone was quarried in Over Stowey for building by 1614 and in the nineteenth century there were quarries at Adscombe, which produced a fireplace for Dunster Castle, and further south, where a rare green igneous rock, formerly known as Schalstein, was used in the construction of Quantock Lodge and to make the pillars for Buckland St Mary church.[58] Roadstone was extracted in many areas during the nineteenth and early twentieth centuries and malachite was said to have been found in such a quarry at Pepperhill c. 1920. One of the most commonly dug types of rock however was limestone which was quarried and burnt wherever it could be found, but notably in Aisholt where in 1652 one woman was licensed to operate a kiln for three years. Quarries and a kiln at Hawkridge continued in use until the 1930s and kilns can still be seen by the roadside in several places.

Copper is said to have been extracted at Bincombe between 1690 and 1724 and licences to mine on Aley manor were granted in 1720 and at Friarn manor in Bincombe in 1755 and 1758. A mine possibly on Dodington lands was operating near Walford's Gibbet by 1790. This northern part of the Quantocks was the most important area for mineral extraction, especially around Holford and Dodington where copper mining began in the early years of the eighteenth century employing miners from Cornwall and Northern England. Landowners reserved mineral rights which they let to speculative investors like the Taunton tobacconist who took an exploration lease in 1757. Regular mining was at

*Right: Engine house, Dodington copper mine.*
S.C.C. ENVIRONMENT DEPT.

*Enmore castle, once the heart of the Earl of Egmont's estate. Following a series of ruinous lawsuits the whole property was put up for sale in 1833. Five thousand acres were sold as a single unit for £135,000 to Henry Labouchere, who added them to his Quantock estate. Much of the castle was subsequently demolished.*

SOMERSET COUNTY COUNCIL.

its height in the final decades of the eighteenth century when ore from the area was exported. By the early nineteenth century local people had obviously tired of the business and there were complaints of unrailed shafts and nuisances from ore dressing. The rector of Dodington refused to allow a steam pumping engine to be built on his land and despite an attempt at revival by Thomas Poole the mines were finally abandoned in the 1820s. Property offered for sale included the assay office and counting house.[60]

Veins of copper said to stretch throughout the Quantocks led to several landowners trying to mine on their land but without success. In Broomfield Andrew Crosse attempted to mine copper at Wort Wood between the 1820s and 1850s with Cornish miners and engineers but the mines were constantly flooded. Around 1825 a 30-metre adit and two shafts were opened but they filled with water. In 1845 the mine was reopened using a steam engine but work was abandoned as the engine was not sufficiently powerful to cope with the amount of water in the mine. In 1852 the Broomfield Consols Copper and Silver-Lead Mining Company was formed with offices in Taunton and London to resume mining, this time working three mines named in the Cornish fashion after local landowners and their wives. But claims of the discovery of ores of copper, lead, malachite and silver may have been fraudulent and mining was abandoned in 1854. A mine at Merridge is said to have produced iron, copper and malachite, probably the same one said to have produced copper and silver in 1870. Mineral fever among local landowners in the nineteenth century probably only lined the pockets of unscrupulous surveyors and others. Sulphur ore was certainly found at Merridge, however, and was sold to a manure works in Wiltshire to make oil of vitriol.[61]

The Quantock hills have also been used for recreation. Thomas Poole's literary friends and the Revd William Holland may have thought they had nothing in common but both enjoyed a walk on the Quantocks. Carriage drives were built by wealthy landowners in the nineteenth century so that they might enjoy the fresh air and scenic views without getting too much exercise. They also enjoyed extensive shooting and hunting rights, especially in the later nineteenth century on the Cothelstone and Quantock estates. During our own era people flee our over-populated towns and cities looking for peace and safe walking on the hills, unfortunately often in such numbers that they could be forgiven for thinking all their fellow citizens had accompanied them, and giving rise to that most recent addition to the archaeology of the Quantocks – the car park!

*The Quantock coast at St Audries – a favoured spot for those fleeing 'our over-populated towns and cities'.*

S.C.C. ENVIRONMENT DEPT.

*Seasonal changes in the colour and texture of the hills make the Quantocks attractive to visitors in both summer and winter – Sheppard's Combe.*

ALL ILLUSTRATIONS IN THIS CHAPTER ARE BY COURTESY OF S.C.C. ENVIRONMENT DEPT.

# IV

# Exploitation to Heritage Management – the Twentieth Century

The appreciation of natural beauty is not confined to any one period of history. No doubt Tom Poole's literary friends took as much pleasure from their perambulations on the hill as today's ramblers. But the enjoyment of such things is a feature of more prosperous times when people are released from the daily grind of subsistence.

This century has seen a steady increase in leisure-time and personal mobility, and the pressures on wild and beautiful places have grown as a consequence. The Quantock Hills had provided a subsistence living for a small local population, and the pleasure grounds of the wealthy landowners. The advent of the motor car very rapidly brought the area within reach of those seeking escape from the confines of nearby towns, and, as the century has progressed, the catchment of potential visitors has grown larger each year.

The process was accentuated by the increasingly intensive use of the enclosed lowlands, giving a greater rarity value to large expanses of open unfenced coutryside. Here people felt they could roam, more or less at will; and nature, albeit modified by centuries of human activity, could still be enjoyed. The Quantocks also possessed another great asset, a perception of 'wildness', perhaps being the first place where this could be experienced in any journey westward from the capital. It is largely an

*'The perception of wildness' – Stert and Somerton Combes.*

illusion, of course, and the intrepid adventure-seeker has the security of knowing that going downhill in any direction will quickly re-establish contact with civilisation!

Photographic and documentary evidence[62] show clearly that the effects of visitor pressures were already visible before the war, and rapidly increased in the immediate post-war years. The same was happening elsewhere, and the growth of national concern that heritage landscapes needed protective legislation led to a spate of reports in the 1940s.[63] The Dower Report identified land outside the newly-proposed National Parks where the landscape was considered to be nationally important, and the subsequent Hobhouse Report translated these into 'Conservation Areas' to be regarded as an 'essential corollary' to the proposed National Parks. They were areas which it was thought did not call for the degree of positive management required in National Parks, but in which it was important for special measures to be taken to preserve their beauty and interest. Generally those areas were less wild than National Parks, and their more intensive land use did not permit so much freedom of access. One of those areas was the Quantock Hills, and when the recommendations of those reports became legislation in 1949[64] the Hills were on the short-list to become what was now defined as an 'Area of Outstanding Natural Beauty' (AONB).

It was not until 1965 that the first AONB's were designated in England and Wales, and the Quantock Hills was the first in England to be so recognised. Designation under the Act followed prolonged negotiation between the National Parks Commission (now the Countryside Commission) and the local authorities, and obviously the definition of the boundary of the Area was the major issue. In the event, the designation covered 38 square miles from Kingston St Mary in the south to the coast in the north. Wherever possible, fixed features on the ground were used to define the boundary, and much of the line on the map uses roads, such as the A358 between West Bagborough and Bicknoller. There has never been any subsequent significant pressure to change the boundary, which in places is very arbitrary, and excludes areas which most would call 'Quantock country'. Nevertheless, we must assume that they got it about right. The AONB encompasses land in 17 parishes, and since local government reorganisation in 1974, 3 District Council areas.

The effect of designation was to place upon the local authorities an obligation to preserve and enhance the natural beauty of the Area. This obligation has been expanded and refined through subsequent legislation, Government policy statements and guidance. In 1956, therefore, the Quantock Hills was officially recognised as being part of the national landscape heritage, and its safeguarding was entrusted to the local councils. There was no special requirement to cater for the

needs of visitors; this being the major difference from the new National Parks such as Exmoor, in which the promotion of enjoyment by the public was an objective.

So what were the post-war Quantocks like? What changes were taking place, what were the threats to this cherished 'natural beauty'? More importantly, what powers did the local authorities have to carry out their new obligations?

The land remained in the ownership of those who held it before; the state took no new powers in this respect. Common land remained common, later to be defined and registered under a new Act in 1965.[65] The area designated as the AONB was roughly one third enclosed farmland, around the fringe of the main hill area; one-third woodland and forestry, in three large blocks and many fragmented pieces; and one-third open heathland, in one main block with a few outlying fragments. This pattern of land-use was a reflection of what had gone before, and is described earlier. But while changing economic and political fortune has always dictated the fate of marginal land – coming in and out of cultivation as need arose – large parts of the Quantocks have remained comparatively constant, in land use terms, for centuries. The main differences have been a matter of degree – the intensity of grazing on the commons, or rate of felling in the woodlands for example. Continuity of this type normally produces valuable wildlife sites, and the Quantocks are no exception. Now over 2500ha is notified as a Site of Special Scientific Interest[66] as one of the most extensive areas of semi-natural habitat in South West England.

*Visitor surveys are essential to understanding how the public use the hills.*

What was changing was the intensity of public usage of the Hills – a perception in some minds of motor bikes, litter, poaching and vandalism taking over from the grasping landlord as the main threat to the well-being of the Quantocks, its people and wildlife. It is always easy to blame 'outsiders' for problems, but the facts show something different. Visitor surveys in 1973 and 1987 showed that almost three-quarters of the public hill users were local, in the sense that they came from within a half hour's drive away.[67] What is more, almost one-third made regular visits, at least once a month. The vast majority arrived by car, as many as 700 cars being on the hill at peak times. In the 1960s the County Council had responded to this pressure by constructing small, discreet car parks at Lydeard Hill, Triscombe Stone and Dead Woman's Ditch. Many other informal parking areas already existed, such as at Cothelstone Hill, Crowcombe Park Gate and Staple Plain. What was most apparent was the extent of vehicular access to the open hill land. Aerial photographs portrayed dramatically what was evident on the ground – miles of eroded trackways across the hills, often in places where no public rights for vehicles existed. Expressions of concern were growing, and by the early 1970s, abuse of the area by vehicles had become the single biggest issue confronting the local authorities and landowners alike. Remedies were not straightforward, and the issue was further complicated by

*Left: Hunt-followers' vehicles – Thorncombe Hill.*

*Visitors at Crowcombe Combe Gate.*

*Right: Triscombe Quarry.*

claims and counter-claims concerning the activities of the followers in vehicles of the Quantock Staghounds, who met three times, and later twice, a week throughout the winter period when the ground was wet and vegetation dormant.

Traffic growth of another kind was also implicated in the other main issue, that of the steady reduction in commoners' grazing stock on the hill. Most of the common had some sort of fence or boundary around its perimeter, but roads provided convenient bolt-holes for straying sheep and ponies, and the busy A39 which crosses the edge of the common near Holford was becoming a killing-ground for commoners' stock. The effect of reduced grazing was scrub invasion of the heath, a process almost imperceptible in the short-term but recognisable from comparative aerial photographs. Combined with the insidious spread of the alien rhododendron into the woodlands and across the heath, the natural beauty of the Quantocks was perceived to be under threat.

Finally, the other major threat identifiable in the 1950s was the prospect of the hills being quarried away for roadstone. Small quarries for building-stone had long been a feature of the landscape, but as demand rose in the post-war road building era, sources of high quality roadstone were at a premium. Two major working quarries, at Triscombe and St Audries, were exploiting the Hangman Grit, valuable

*The A39 at Holford – the problem of a busy main road crossing the edge of a grazing common.*

for surface-dressing roads, and several other minor quarries had valid consent with potential for expansion. Thankfully, a combination of geological problems, a down-turn in the economy, and the recognition of the sensitivity of mineral working in an AONB conspired to reduce the threat. Activity is now confined to a single working unit at Triscombe, where new owners have carried out major environmental improvements.

The duties laid on the local authorities by the 1949 Act made action to address these problems essential. Firstly, the administrative arrangements were put in place in 1974, when the new District Councils of Sedgemoor, Taunton Deane and West Somerset joined the County Council in setting up a Joint Advisory Committee (JAC) to oversee Quantock affairs. Although the new body had no executive powers, it could bring issues to the attention of each authority, with a request for the necessary action. The JAC's first act was to recommend the creation of a warden service to take action on the ground. The first warden was appointed in 1976, his post half-funded by the Government through the Countryside Commission, and the four local councils sharing the balance. Now, for the first time, the authorites had regular contact with landowners, farmers, commoners, local residents and visitors. Problems and issues could be identified more accurately and solutions sought.

The need for some form of management plan for the hills was recognised early in JAC's deliberations. The planning process is a complex affair, and has been the subject of regular changes. In 1968, a new Act[68] introduced the system of County Structure Plans dealing with strategic planning issues, and Local Plans, which within the guidelines of the Structure Plan defined detailed proposals for particular areas. In Somerset's other AONB, the Mendip Hills, a Local Plan was prepared jointly with Avon County Council for the designated AONB, a novel and unique solution to the particular problem of that area. That form of plan was not appropriate for the Quantocks, so the decision was taken to prepare a non-statutory Management Plan which could address detailed land management issues not considered appropriate for inclusion in Local Plans.

A characteristic of Somerset people has always been an unwillingness to have new ideas suddenly thrust upon them. Today's planning system, with a high level of public participation, was well-suited to the problems of the Quantocks, and the County Council took on the role of co-ordinating the views of all the local interests to fashion the plan. What may seem to have been a long drawn-out process was valuable in that through the many meetings, both public and private, an opportunity was provided for everyone to have their say.

*Left: Warden Service at work tree planting.*

## The Quantock Hills Management Plan[69].

First and foremost, the plan set out to conserve the natural beauty and historic heritage of the AONB. Secondly it sought to balance the land use demands on the Area, and thirdly to tackle the problems of common land management.

To achieve these objectives, almost 40 proposals are set out; some simple and straightforward, some complex and involving further negotiation. The plan did not deal with issues such as the control of development, a matter for District Council Local Plans, or the social structure of the villages, which is outside planning control. But all these things are interlinked – the rapid growth of peripheral villages like Bishops Lydeard and Nether Stowey in the 1970s and 80s had increased local pressures on nearby hill land. Similarly the trend for retired folk to settle in attractive villages like Bicknoller, Holford and St Audries, and a steady increase in second homes in the area, have had effects. Those people have selected the area for its natural beauty, and generally have the time to take advantage of it. Some examples will demonstrate the ways in which intervention management is now a feature of twentieth century society's requirement for national heritage land.

*Bicknoller.*

The common land, that vestige of land tenure and society's needs of earlier times, is a crucial element in the future of the Quantocks. Its common status is one reason why the hills have retained their character. An example of how things might have been different is Quantock Farm, created in the late seventeenth century, as the manorial system was breaking up, and still there today as an island of enclosed grassland in a sea of heathland and woodland. The farm's non-common status also attracted attention in 1972, when it was proposed for a championship golf course. Happily, after a public inquiry, the then Secretary of State ruled that such developments, with their attendant car parking and accommodation requirements, would be out of keeping with the character of the Quantocks AONB.

The Commons Registration Act in 1965 established the boundaries and rights attached to today's common land. The main block is north of Great Wood, and includes parish 'customs commons' attached to Over and Nether Stowey. To the south, Wills Neck and Aisholt Common are outliers of this block covered under the same registration, and there are separate registrations for Merridge Hill, Broomfield and Broomfield Hill Common. Rights registered vary. The principal one is the right of pasture, with over 40 entries for a total of almost 5000 animals, mainly

*Grazing stock on the common – Dowsborough.*

*Heathland management through controlled burning.*

sheep, but including ponies, cattle and goats. Clearly the grazing cannot support this number of animals, and other mechanisms ensure that the carrying capacity of about 1300 sheep is not exceeded. In reality, however, the trend continues downwards, as a combination of straying problems and the sale of peripheral land to which rights are attached. Few newcomers to these peripheral farms have shown interest in exercising their traditional grazing rights on the commons, though many are interested in the future management of the land. If the heathland is not grazed it has to be maintained in other ways, for example burning – a traditional activity now revised under the plan – and cutting by machine. The alternative is the progressive invasion of scrub and a resultant change in the visual character, access opportunities and wildlife value. Heathland of this type is now a precious wildlife resource in England, and the few remaining fragments have become a priority for protection and sympathetic management. A Commons Management Group, set up under the plan now prepares proposals for the common and liaises with landowners and the Commoners Association to help safeguard this resource.

The other main rights registered are for estovers (mainly the cutting of small wood or underwood for fuel) and turbary (the cutting of turf or peat for fuel). Occasionally the exercise of the right to cut wood causes conflict when fly-by-night chainsaw merchants move in illegally to fell trees, for example on the customs commons. Happily, one beneficial consequence of recent winter storms has been a surfeit of available firewood, and illegal activities have much reduced. Turbary rights have not been exercised in recent times, principally because there is insufficient peat or turf to make it worthwhile.

One of the great benefits of common land status in Britain is the legal obligation that the land will not be fenced. The result on the Quantocks is the large expanses of open land so characteristic of the area. A fence of sorts has, however, existed at the boundary of the common since the enclosures. The plan sought to close the gaps in this fence, and to construct new sections, such as along the A39 at Holford, where straying stock and a busy road co-exist to the hazard of both animals and road-users. This has been a contentious issue, and continues to be opposed by some as an erosion of the ancient requirement that commons should remain unfenced. The owner of the land in question is the National Trust, and it is the intention of the Trust at the time of writing to pursue an application to deal with this problem.

There is much public misconception about the rights attached to common land. There is a significant difference between urban commons,

*Worn tracks have shown remarkable powers of recovery once vehicles are removed – Cothelstone Hill.*

*Ancient semi-natural woodland – Holford Combe.*

which are generally freely available for public access, and the majority of Quantocks commons where such rights do not exist. However, de facto access is available over much of the land, and is supported by an extensive network of public rights of way. Unfortunately there are always the few who assume more, and those who choose to use vehicles to obtain access have been a major problem in the Quantocks for many years. Vehicular rights of way do exist on the hills, and the plan seeks to confine vehicle-users to these tracks, or others where owners have given consent to their use. Elsewhere, off-road driving is discouraged, and prosecutions are brought against persistent offenders. The effect of these measures has been startling, and deeply-eroded tracks, with help, have greened-up rapidly in recent years. The role of the warden service in operating this control is essential.

It is interesting how folk-memory of commons affairs has been handed-down through the generations. In 1837 commoners at Merridge Hill had major problems with the landowner, 'Squire' Esdaile of Cothelstone. When the County Council bought the land in 1973 and tried to control the vehicular damage occurring on Cothelstone Hill, objections by the commons-rights holders were accompanied by detailed accounts of that dispute. The new landlord was obviously viewed in the same light as Esdaile 140 years previously – grasping and untrustworthy. The plan, and the process of its preparation, tries to erase those unhappy memories and establish new and co-operative working arrangements to safeguard the interests of commoners and landowners alike.

Some of the Quantock woodlands are also common land, presenting problems of management and natural regeneration where grazing stock are concerned. Current stocking-levels of sheep and ponies do not put undue pressure on the woods, even when combined with the effects of deer-browsing, but the ideal headage to keep the heathland grazed to an appropriate level may well cause problems in some woodland areas. Temporary enclosures to exclude stock and allow the natural regeneration of trees to proceed may well have to be negotiated. Such measures inevitably raise suspicions about internal sub-division of the commons with some people, and have to be handled sensitively.

Elsewhere, many of the Quantock woodlands display signs of the management practices of former times. Extensive felling of timber in war-time, and for major building projects, was not always accompanied by appropriate replanting and management. In the nineteenth century quicker-growing conifers were replacing the native hardwoods and the process accelerated dramatically after the First World War when Great Wood, the former Stanley Estate, was leased to the Forestry Commission and extensively re-stocked as a conifer plantation. Other new plantations were established at Wind Down, at Buncombe and Cothelstone and on

*Conifer plantation – Buncombe.*

the former Deer Park at Stowborrow Hill. In fifty years the landscape was changed very significantly in those areas, and changes continue as the plantations are reaching felling-age and large blocks of clear-fell are created. The plan seeks, within commercial management constraints, to promote the progressive return of these areas to native broadleaved woodland, and to ensure that all existing broadleaved woodland is properly managed and maintained as broadleaved.

The Quantock woodlands have been a precious resource for centuries – important local sources of timber, fuel, charcoal and tanning products. They are no less valuable today, both in commercial terms and for the wildlife and amenity needs of the twenty-first century. Parts of the woodland cover have been continuous as far back as records allow us to see, and such ancient semi-natural woods – fragments of the original wildwood cover – have become a national priority for conservation. Only 5.6% of Somerset is wooded, and, of that, less than a quarter is classed as ancient semi-natural.[70] In Britain almost half of the ancient woods have been lost since 1930, the majority to coniferous plantations. In the Quantocks that process seems to have started much earlier.

Just as the woodlands provide historical continuity, the archaeological and historic features of the Quantocks are vitally important. All landscapes, particularly in these crowded islands, have been modified by centuries of human activity, but it is in the wilder, remoter areas that the evidence remains least damaged by the pressures of intensive land-use. A recent survey[71] has revealed further sites of archaeological interest in the hills, to add to the previously-recorded 268 sites. Earlier records were mainly of the more obvious landscape features, such as barrows, cairns, mounds and hillforts. The new research has revealed many other features such as enclosures, flint-scatters and deserted farmsteads.

Some of these sites may in due course become Ancient Monuments, protected under legislation[72] as being of national importance and adding to the existing 48 such sites in the Quantock Hills. Others will be recorded as county monuments where protection is obtained through negotiation and agreement. The pressure of recreational use in the hills is a constant threat to fragile surface evidence of this type and many such features show signs of erosion through foot, hoof and vehicle. On-site management through the Warden Service is crucial to minimise these threats.

Finally, what of the future? We must assume that recreational pressures will grow inexorably for reasons stated earlier, and in the light of continuing agricultural surpluses, marginal land will become more important for heritage than economic reasons. The local authorities, through the Structure Plan, Local Plans and the Management Plan have signalled their commitment to protect and manage this beautiful area for the benefit of the present and future generations. More and more this process will be achieved through co-operation, understanding and partnership between Government agencies, the local authorities, landowners, farmers, rights-holders and local residents. The Management Plan proposes an Agreement between the main parties to support its measures and their implementation. It is hoped that such agreement will be progressively forthcoming in future years.

# References

Only a selection of references is given here. Readers interested in sources for other statements will find them for Bicknoller, Crowcombe, Dodington, Holford, Nether Stowey, Kilton, Kilve, and East and West Quantoxhead in *Victoria History of Somerset*, v, ed. R W Dunning (1985), and for most of the remainder of the Quantock parishes in *Victoria History of Somerset*, vi, ed. R W Dunning (forthcoming).

1  E Ekwall, *Oxford Dictionary of English Place-Names*.

2  R R J McDonnell, *The Quantock Hills . . . An Archaeological Survey* (Somerset County Planning Department 1989).

3  L V Grinsell, *The Archaeology of Exmoor: Bideford Bay to Bridgwater* (1970); L V Grinsell, *Prehistoric Sites in the Quantock Country* (Somerset Archaeological and Natural History Society 1976, revised 1991).

4  S (omerset) R (ecord) O (ffice), DD/SAS C/923.

5  Ibid. DD/X/WI 34.

6  *Victoria History of Somerset*, ii, ed. W Page (1911), 553-4.

7  *Book of Fees*, i. 84.

8  For information on a second William de Falaise see M Baylé, 'Les Chapiteaux de Stogursey (Somerset) ...' in *Bulletin Monumental*, 138 (1980), 405-6.

9  *Stogursey Charters* (Somerset Record Society lxi), p 1.

10  MS collection of Sir William Pole (known as Pole MS), of which a photocopy is held in the Victoria History Office, County Hall, Taunton, charter no 2957.

11  P (ublic) R (ecord) O (ffice), E 142/8.

12  PRO SC6/974/8.

13  Eton College Records 49/272; Alnwick Castle MSS, X.II.12.9a (iii).

14  PRO SC6/1090/4.

15  West Sussex RO, Petworth House Archives, MAC uncatalogued.

16  *Cartulary of St Mark's Hospital, Bristol* (Bristol Record Society xxi), p 160.

17  W H P Greswell, 'The Quantocks and their Place-Names' *Proceedings of the Somerset Archaeological and Natural History Society*, xlvi, 125-48.

18  *Stogursey Charters*, p 19.

19  *Somerset Pleas* (Somerset Record Society xi), 23.

20  *Somerset Wills* (Somerset Record Society xvi), 29.

21  *Wells Wills*, ed. F W Weaver, 82.

22  *Wells Cathedral Manuscripts*, i. 514, 518-19; SRO, DD/AH 64/5.

23  Dorset RO, D/WLC/M244.

24  *Calendar of Patent Rolls 1354–8*, 616.

25  SRO, DD/AH 11/9.

26  *Feet of Fines, Henry IV to Henry VI* (Somerset Record Society xxii), 118.

27  *The Hylle Cartulary* (Somerset Record Society lxviii); PRO, SC6/977/1-2, 5, 8, 11, 13, 16, 18, 20, 22-3; 1119/17; Hen VII/549-52.

28  *Victoria History of Somerset*, v, 16.

29  SRO, DD/X/WI 34.

30  Ibid. DD/AH 11/10; DD/S/WH 209.

31  Ibid. DD/WG, box 16.

32  PRO, WARD 2/28/70/11.

33  PRO, E 178/5623; SRO, DD/S/SH (N/153).

34  SRO, DD/HC (N/28); DD/SAS (C/923), map 1688.

35  *Paupers and Pigkillers: the Diary of William Holland, a Somerset Parson 1799-1818*, ed J Ayres (1984), passim.

36  SRO, DD/CH 88/4.

37  *Victoria History of Somerset*, v, 60.

38  SRO, DD/S/WH 41, 246.

39  Alnwick Castle MSS.

40  SRO, DD/S/WH 256.

41  Ibid. DD/11/1; DD/PLE 63.

42  Ibid. DD/DHR box 36, map 1744; DD/X/BB 6; Bristol RO 4490, 04237.

43  *Paupers and Pigkillers*, 185, 230, 235, 254.

44  SRO, tithe award, Over Stowey.

45  *Rep. Com. Employment in Agric.* p 125, (HC 1843), xii.

46  *Rep. Com. Employment in Agric.* p 482, (HC 1868-9), xiii.

47  SRO, DD/SP inventory 1641.

48  *Proceedings of the Somerset Archaeological and Natural History Society*, xliv, 22-8.

49  SRO, DD/AH 34/22; Q/SR 121/13.

50  *Paupers and Pigkillers*, 270, 274.

51  *Quarter Sessions Records, Charles I* (Somerset Record Society, xxiv), 137.

52  SRO, Q/SR 115/131.

53  Ibid. DD/SP inventory 1688.

54  Ibid. 1716.

55  *Taunton Courier*, 28 March 1832.

56  *Victoria History of Somerset*, v, 4.

57  Ibid. 60.

58  SRO, DD/X/WI 34; *Proceedings of the Somerset Archaeological and Natural History Society*, xliii, 11.

59  SRO, DD/WG 7/9; DD/X/HAM 1.

60  *Victoria History of Somerset*, v, 67.

61  SRO, DD/S/WH 326; DD/X/HAM 1.

62  Somerset County Council – Aerial Surveys 1971, 1981 and selected earlier cover. Held in Department for the Environment, County Hall, Taunton.

63  (1) Report of the Committee on Land Utilization in Rural Areas, Cmd 6378 HMSO 1942 ("The Scott Report").

    (2) National Parks in England and Wales, Cmd 6628 HMSO 1945 ("The Dower Report").

    (3) Report of the National Parks Committee (England and Wales) Cmd 7121 HMSO 1947 ("The Hobhouse Report").

64  National Parks and Access to the Countryside Act 1949.

65  Commons Registration Act 1965.

66  Under S.28 of the Wildlife and Countryside Act 1981. Notified in 1986.

67  (1) Quantock Hills Visitor Survey 1973. (Somerset County Council (unpublished)).

    (2) Quantock Hills Visitor Survey 1987. (Somerset County Council, May 1988).

68  Town and County Planning Act 1968.

69  Quantock Hills Management Plan. (Somerset County Council 1988).

70  (1) Census of Woodlands and Trees 1978-82 – County of Somerset. (Forestry Commission 1983).

    (2) G A Lister and A L Pinches, *Somerset – Inventory of Ancient Woodland* (Nature Conservancy Council 1986).

71  R R J McDonnell, *The Quantock Hills* 1989.

72  Ancient Monuments and Archaeological Areas Act 1979.